W9-BSW-645

INTERNATIONAL SPACE STATION

THE SCIENCE LAB IN SPACE

By John Hamilton

SPACECRAFT

A&D Xtreme
An Imprint of Abdo Publishing | abdopublishing.com

abdopublishing.com

Published by Abdo Publishing, a division of ABDO, PO Box 398166, Minneapolis, Minnesota 55439. Copyright ©2018 by Abdo Consulting Group, Inc. International copyrights reserved in all countries. No part of this book may be reproduced in any form without written permission from the publisher. A&D Xtreme™ is a trademark and logo of Abdo Publishing.

Printed in the United States of America, North Mankato, MN.
032017
052017

Editor: Sue Hamilton
Graphic Design: Sue Hamilton
Cover Design: Candice Keimig
Cover Photo: iStock
Interior Photos: All photos NASA.

Websites
To learn more about Xtreme Spacecraft, visit abdobooklinks.com. These links are routinely monitored and updated to provide the most current information available.

Publisher's Cataloging-in-Publication Data

Names: Hamilton, John, author.
Title: International space station: the science lab in space / by John Hamilton.
Other titles: Science lab in space
Description: Minneapolis, MN : Abdo Publishing, 2018. | Series: Xtreme spacecraft | Includes index.
Identifiers: LCCN 2016962226 | ISBN 9781532110085 (lib. bdg.) | ISBN 9781680787931 (ebook)
Subjects: LCSH: International Space Station--Juvenile literature. | Space stations--
    Juvenile literature.
Classification: DDC 629.4--dc23
LC record available at http://lccn.loc.gov/2016962226

CONTENTS

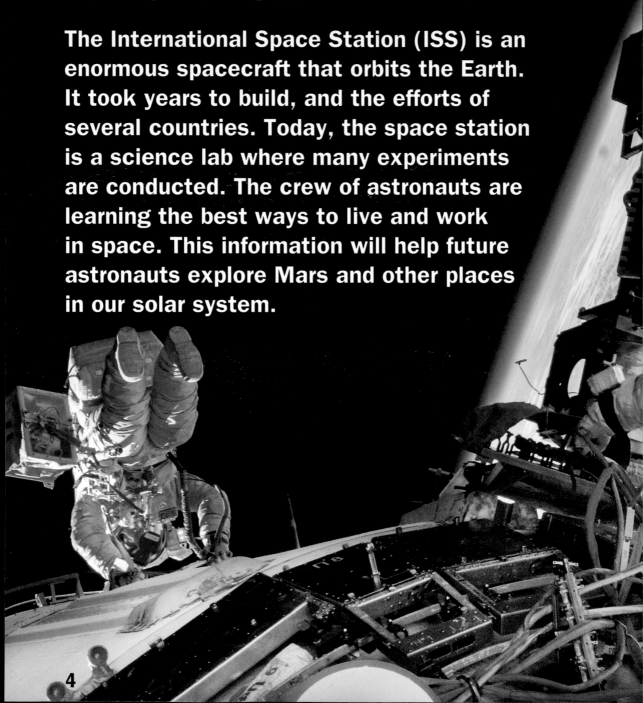

THE SCIENCE LAB IN SPACE

The International Space Station (ISS) is an enormous spacecraft that orbits the Earth. It took years to build, and the efforts of several countries. Today, the space station is a science lab where many experiments are conducted. The crew of astronauts are learning the best ways to live and work in space. This information will help future astronauts explore Mars and other places in our solar system.

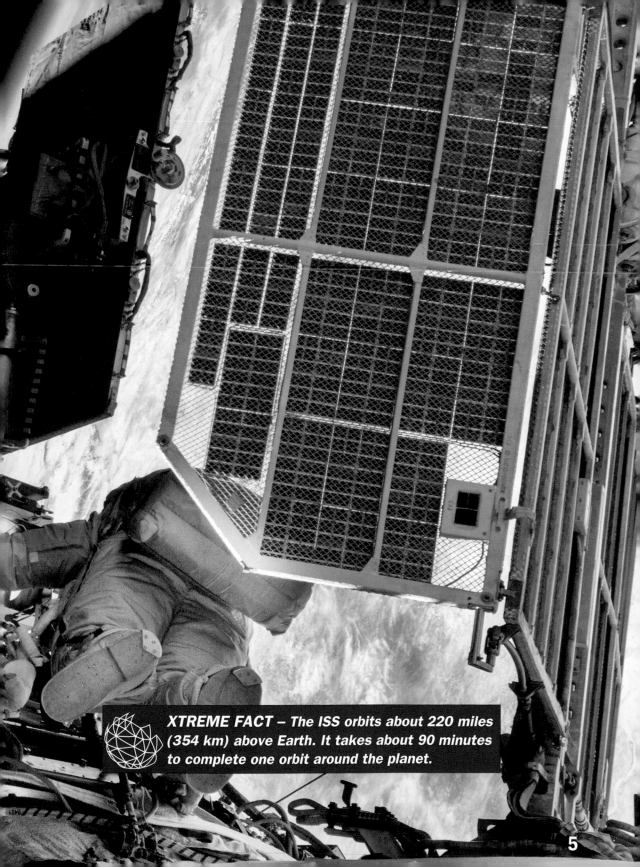

XTREME FACT – *The ISS orbits about 220 miles (354 km) above Earth. It takes about 90 minutes to complete one orbit around the planet.*

SPACE STATION HISTORY

Space stations are spacecraft that orbit the Earth for months or years. Salyut 1 was the first space station. It was put in orbit by the Soviet Union in 1971.

Salyut 7 was put in orbit in 1982.

The United States launched its first space station in 1973. It was called Skylab. It orbited the Earth until 1979.

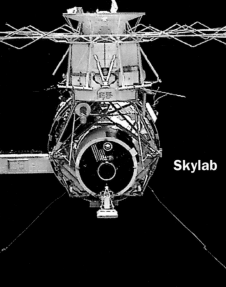

Skylab

The first part of Russia's Mir space station was launched in 1986. It was built in sections. It orbited until 2001. The lessons learned from these early spacecraft were later used to help build the International Space Station.

Mir

XTREME FACT – In 2011, China launched a small space station named Tiangong-1. It was followed by Tiangong-2 in 2016. A larger modular Chinese space station is planned for 2020.

BUILDING THE ISS

The ISS took years to plan and the help of 15 nations. The station's five main partners include NASA from the United States, together with space agencies from Russia, Europe, Canada, and Japan.

The modules Zarya (left) and Unity (right) are shown docked together in December 1998.

Russia launched the first piece of the ISS, called Zarya, into orbit in 1998. An American module, called Unity, was connected a few weeks later. Dozens of modules have been added in the years since. The modules were brought to the ISS by Russian rockets and NASA's fleet of space shuttles.

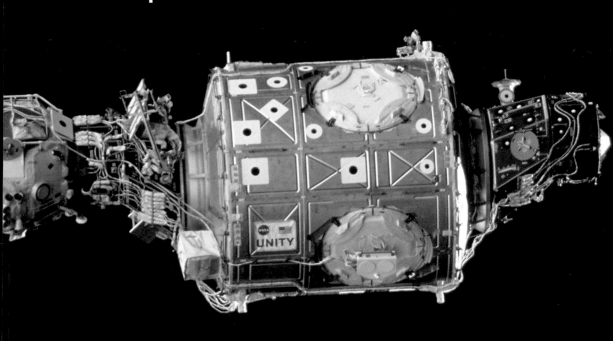

 XTREME FACT – *It took more than 115 space flights to bring all the pieces needed to construct the ISS, at a cost of about $100 billion.*

The first long-term crew to live aboard the ISS arrived in 2000. They were Sergei Krikalev and Yuri Gidzenko of Russia and William Shepherd of the United States. People have lived on the ISS ever since.

Over the next several years, many crews from different nations put together the pieces of the space

The Zvezda service module being built in Russia in 1997.

station. They added living quarters, science laboratories, solar panels, and other modules.

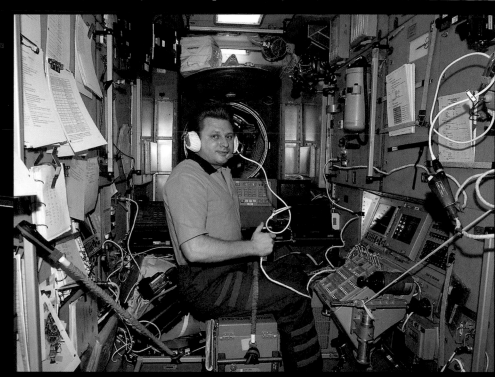

Cosmonaut Yury Onufrienko uses a communication system in the Zvezda service module on the ISS in December 2001.

 XTREME FACT – The ISS is slightly bigger in area than an American football field. If weighed on Earth, it would tip the scales at more than 925,000 pounds (419,573 kg).

RESUPPLY MISSIONS

Fresh crews and supplies are regularly brought to the ISS. During its construction, they arrived by American space shuttles and Russian Soyuz spacecraft. Today, the space shuttle fleet has been retired. Crews return to Earth aboard Soyuz spacecraft.

An unpiloted Progress resupply vehicle approaches the ISS filled with oxygen, water, spare parts, and other items for resident astronauts in November 2011.

A SpaceX Dragon near the ISS's Harmony module.

Other unmanned spacecraft also bring supplies to the ISS. These have included Russian Progress vehicles, American Orbital ATK Cygnus and SpaceX Dragon spacecraft, European ATV spacecraft, and Japanese HTV spacecraft.

XTREME FACT – After Progress spacecraft have been unloaded, astronauts fill the empty space with garbage and unneeded equipment. The spacecraft then undock and fall back to Earth, where they burn up in the atmosphere.

MODULES

The ISS is made of many parts called modules. They are combined and pressurized so astronauts can live and work inside. Some modules are small. Others are nearly as big as a city bus.

Leonardo, a multipurpose module built by the Italian Space Agency, awaits its trip to the ISS.

Cosmonaut Yuri Gidzenko floats inside the Leonardo module filled with hardware for the ISS.

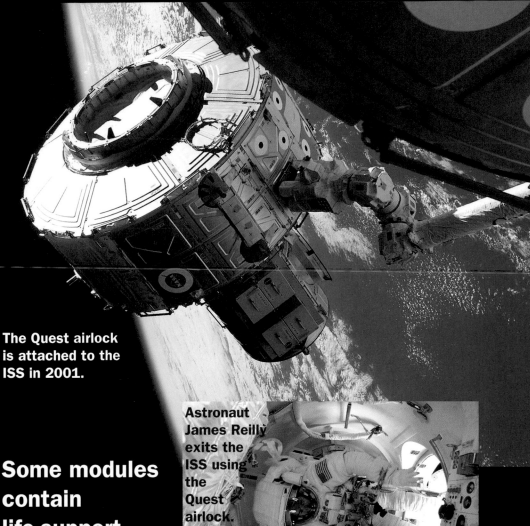

The Quest airlock is attached to the ISS in 2001.

Some modules contain life-support equipment, which provides

Astronaut James Reilly exits the ISS using the Quest airlock.

air and water. Others contain navigation equipment, electrical components, or science experiments. Special modules contain docking ports for other spacecraft. Airlocks are doors that allow astronauts using spacesuits to venture outside.

The Cupola is a dome-shaped module. It is attached to the larger Tranquility module. Built in Italy, the Cupola was attached to the ISS in 2010. Its large windows give astronauts a panoramic view.

Astronaut Alexander Gerst works with the Canadarm2 in the ISS's Cupola in 2014.

XTREME FACT – The Cupola's circular central window is 31.5 inches (80 cm) in diameter. It is the largest window ever used in space.

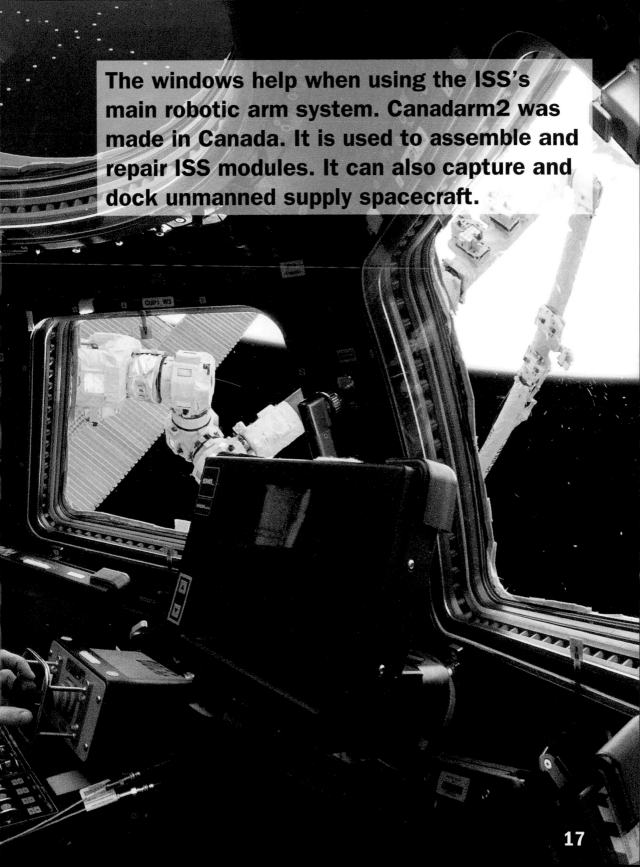

The windows help when using the ISS's main robotic arm system. Canadarm2 was made in Canada. It is used to assemble and repair ISS modules. It can also capture and dock unmanned supply spacecraft.

Astronaut Scott Parazynski repairs one of the ISS's solar arrays in 2006.

SOLAR ARRAYS

The ISS gets its power from large solar arrays. They are made of thousands of solar cells. They absorb energy from the sun and turn it into electricity.

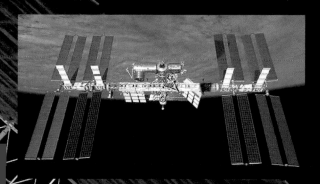

The solar arrays are arranged in four pairs on each side of the space station. When the ISS moves into the Earth's shadow during its 90-minute orbit, sunlight is blocked. During that time, the space station gets its power from rechargeable batteries.

XTREME FACT – Each solar array has a wingspan of 240 feet (73 m), which is longer than the wingspan of a Boeing 777 airliner.

SCIENCE EXPERIMENTS

Space stations today are used mostly for research. Many chemistry, physics, and biology experiments can only be conducted in the weightlessness of space. Science experiments are always underway aboard the ISS.

Astronaut Koichi Wakata floats in the ISS's Kibo lab.

Kibo stands for "hope" in Japanese.

XTREME FACT – The Kibo space laboratory is the single largest module on the ISS. Built in Japan, it is used to conduct research in astronomy, biology, and space medicine.

Scientists also study what happens to the human body after living in space for a long time. This information will be helpful for lengthy future missions.

While astronaut Scott Kelly spent 340 days aboard the ISS from 2015 to 2016, his identical twin brother, astronaut Mark Kelly, stayed on Earth. NASA scientists will compare their health to see if there is any harm to the human body from living in space for so long.

Scott Kelly   Mark Kelly

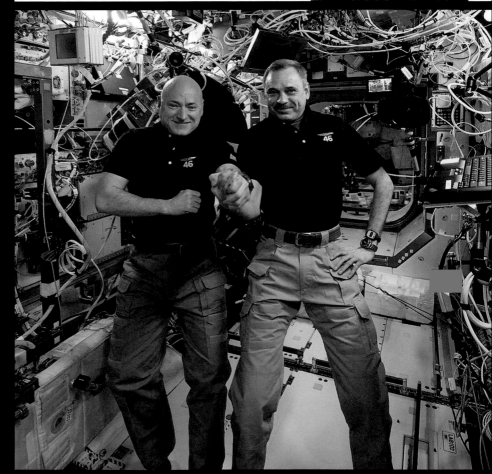

Astronaut Scott Kelly and cosmonaut Mikhail Kornienko shake hands as they complete day 300 of their 340 consecutive days in the ISS in 2016

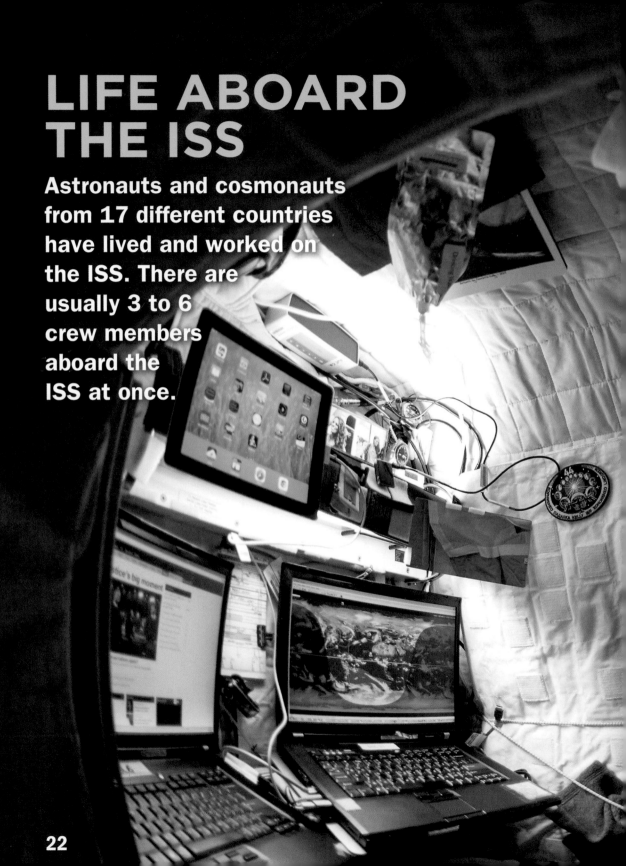

LIFE ABOARD THE ISS

Astronauts and cosmonauts from 17 different countries have lived and worked on the ISS. There are usually 3 to 6 crew members aboard the ISS at once.

Astronauts sleep inside closet-sized cubbies. They crawl inside sleeping bags to give them warmth and to keep them from floating away. After waking, they wash up with moist towels. There are no showers. It is important to keep water bubbles from floating into delicate electronic equipment.

XTREME FACT – ISS missions are called expeditions. Most expeditions last about 6 months.

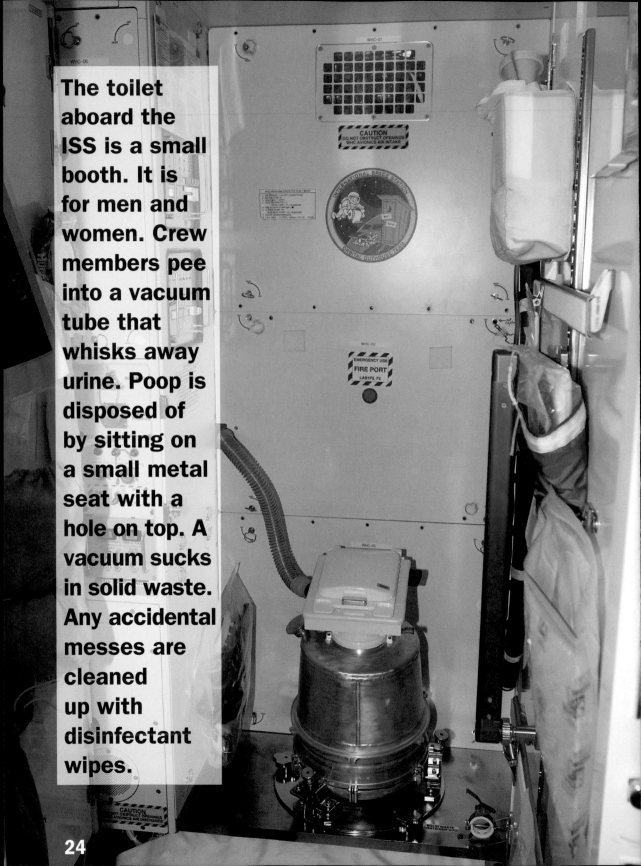

The toilet aboard the ISS is a small booth. It is for men and women. Crew members pee into a vacuum tube that whisks away urine. Poop is disposed of by sitting on a small metal seat with a hole on top. A vacuum sucks in solid waste. Any accidental messes are cleaned up with disinfectant wipes.

Much of the food aboard the ISS is dehydrated. Water must first be added before eating. Water comes in packages with straws on the end.

The food table aboard the ISS in 2015.

Astronauts lose bone density and muscle mass while in space. It is important for them to exercise. They stay in shape by using a treadmill, stationary bike, and weight-lifting machine.

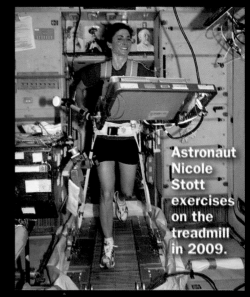

Astronaut Nicole Stott exercises on the treadmill in 2009.

XTREME FACT – The ISS experiences a sunrise every 90 minutes because of its fast orbit. To avoid confusion, crew members keep the same time as mission controllers on Earth.

Astronauts stay very busy. They conduct many science experiments. They also must check, clean, and repair space station equipment. Sometimes the ISS needs repairs on the outside.

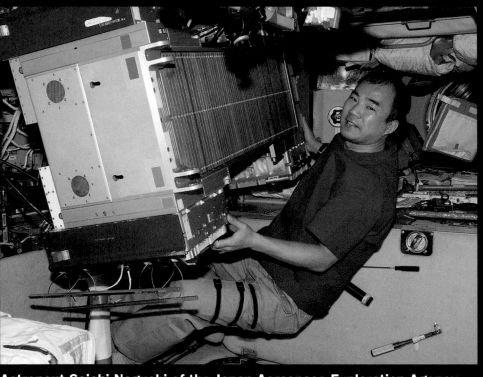

Astronaut Soichi Noguchi of the Japan Aerospace Exploration Agency (JAXA) performs in-flight maintenance on the Treadmill Vibration Isolation System (TVIS) in the Zvezda service module of the ISS.

 XTREME FACT – On Earth, a typical spacesuit weighs about 300 pounds (136 kg). Luckily, the suits don't feel so heavy when astronauts work in the weightlessness of space.

Astronauts put on spacesuits and exit the station through airlocks. Spacewalks are called extravehicular activities (EVAs). They can be dangerous, but are necessary to keep the ISS running in top shape.

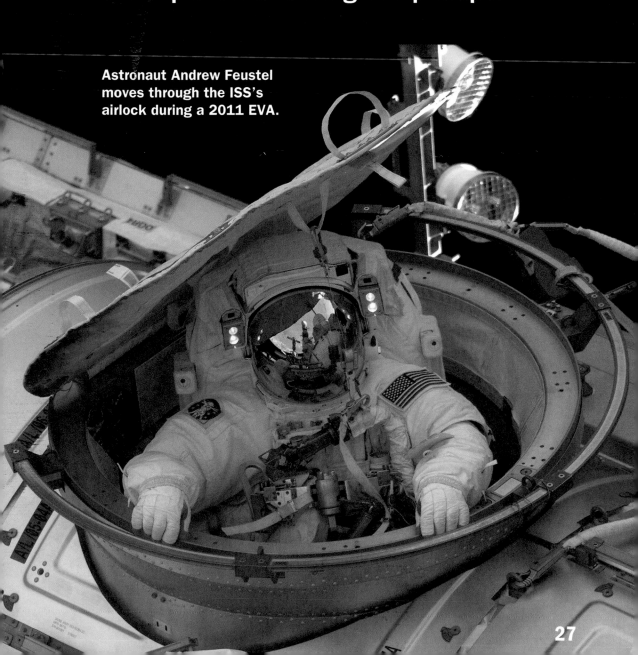

Astronaut Andrew Feustel moves through the ISS's airlock during a 2011 EVA.

FUTURE OF THE ISS

Scientists continue to learn from experiments conducted aboard the ISS. However, the space station will eventually get too old and have to be replaced. For now, NASA expects the ISS to continue operating until the 2020s.

XTREME FACT – At the end of their life-spans, space stations are abandoned and then remotely steered out of orbit. They burn up in the Earth's atmosphere. Some large pieces survive reentry and fall in uninhabited areas, such as the Pacific Ocean.

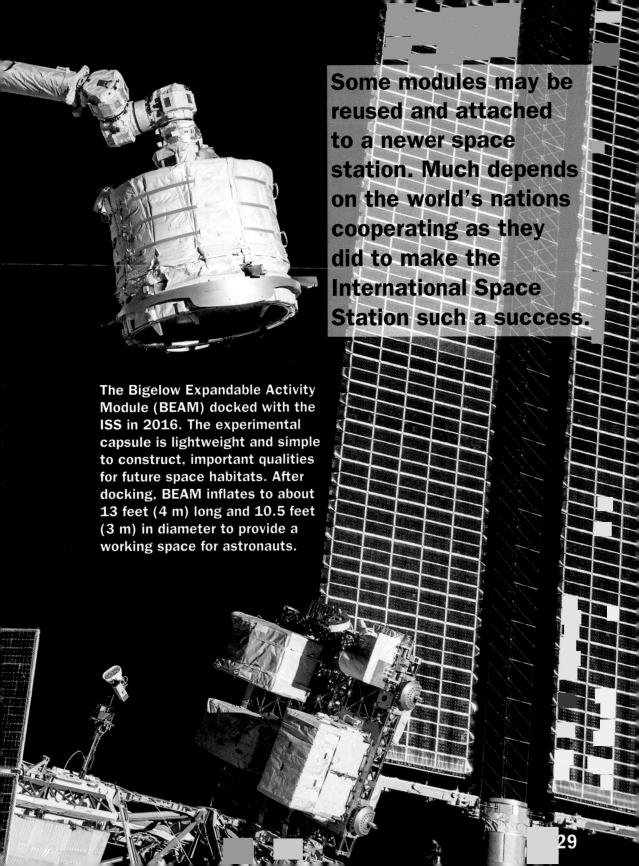

Some modules may be reused and attached to a newer space station. Much depends on the world's nations cooperating as they did to make the International Space Station such a success.

The Bigelow Expandable Activity Module (BEAM) docked with the ISS in 2016. The experimental capsule is lightweight and simple to construct, important qualities for future space habitats. After docking, BEAM inflates to about 13 feet (4 m) long and 10.5 feet (3 m) in diameter to provide a working space for astronauts.

GLOSSARY

COSMONAUT
An astronaut from Russia or the former Soviet Union.

DEHYDRATE
To remove moisture from something. Because the International Space Station doesn't have large refrigerators, many food items are dehydrated to keep them from spoiling while being stored for months at a time.

NATIONAL AERONAUTICS AND SPACE ADMINISTRATION (NASA)
A United States government space agency started in 1958. NASA's goals include space exploration, as well as increasing people's understanding of Earth, our solar system, and the universe.

ORBIT
The circular path a moon or spacecraft makes when traveling around a planet or other large celestial body. The International Space Station takes about 90 minutes to make one complete orbit around the Earth.

SPACE SHUTTLE
America's first
reusable space
vehicle. NASA
built five orbiters:
Columbia,
Challenger,
Atlantis,
Discovery, and
Endeavour.
Two shuttles
and their crews
were destroyed
by accidents:
Challenger
in 1986, and
Columbia in 2003.

SOVIET UNION
A former country
that included a
union of Russia
and several
other communist
republics. It was
formed in 1922
and existed until
1991.

INDEX